# POEMS

## FROM THE

# BLUE RIDGE

*Poems from the Blue Ridge*
Copyright 2017 Alexander H. ter Weele

Published by Piscataqua Press
An imprint of RiverRun Bookstore, Inc.
142 Fleet Street │ Portsmouth, NH │ 03801
www.riverrunbookstore.com
www.piscataquapress.com
ISBN: 978-1-944393-39-7
Printed in the United States of America

# POEMS

## FROM THE

# BLUE RIDGE

*LITTLE SQUAM*
*DREAMS CANNOT THE LIVING TOUCH*
*ONE PATH THROUGH TIME*

*AND MANY MORE POEMS TO MAKE YOU LAUGH, CRY, AND PONDER*

## Alexander H. ter Weele

illustrations by Philippe Grenade xiv

# Acknowledgments

Given the decision to mix text and art, this has been a particularly time-consuming book to edit, format, and print. Without the assistance of Jennifer Dellinger (typist), Elizabeth Barrett (editor), Deborah Bailey (website designer), Tom Holbrook (publisher), and Kellsey Metzger (editorial assistant), it would never have gotten to press. All of them are consummate professionals. In the particular instance of this book, special assistance came from Philippe Grenade XIV, who did the illustrations. One need only riffle through the pages of this book to realize the extent of Grenade's artistic genius. Working with him on this project has been a pleasure. All the artwork in the book is his, but for those few sketches drawn by the author (distinguishable by his signature). Thanks are also due to my daughter France and my friend Pat Wine, who have become my de facto promoters, advertisers, and sales agents. And as always, special thanks go to my wife without whose patience and support, and the coffee she brews, I would accomplish little.

For

# My Wife Francine

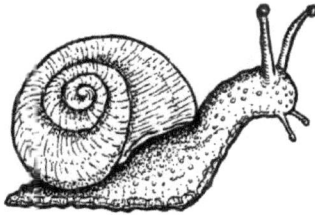

And our children and grandchildren

Kerst, Cathy, Alex, Simonne, Maria, Jan; France,
Daniela, Jakob, Joshua, Kiki;
Eric, Amie, Stafford, Everest; Andre, Katy, Nicolas, Lauren, Margot.

Also by Alexander ter Weele

*We Escaped:*
*A Family's Flight from Holland during World War Two*
Piscataqua Press, 2015

# Foreword

The poems included in this anthology were selected from a larger number of poems written by me during my lifetime. Quite a few were written during the 1960s, a time when I was single and committed to becoming an author. During those years I lived in Delft, the Netherlands, in Beirut, Lebanon, and in Brookfield, New Hampshire. Over that span of ten years, I traveled widely on a motor scooter throughout Europe (the Highlands of Scotland, the firths of Wales, the theaters of London, the parks of Malmo, Tivoli Gardens in Copenhagen, the canals of Amsterdam, bistros in Paris, the Swiss Alps, Luxembourg, Austria, the Italian Lakes Region, beer halls in Germany, Yugoslavia under Tito, the Macedonian mountains in Greece) and throughout the Middle East (the souks of Istanbul, Ephesus, the Krak des Chevaliers, the hubbub of Aleppo, Byblos, Ba'albek and the Bekaa Valley, Tyre, the beaches of Beirut), and then, on snowshoes and in hiking boots I camped in the backwoods of New Hampshire, Maine, and Quebec, fishing, hunting, hiking, canoeing (Mt. Chocorua, Ossipee Lake and the Ossipee Mountains, Winnipesaukee, Magalloway Mountain., the Pine River, the Connecticut Lakes, Mt. Washington, Mt. Katahdin, Moosehead, Nesowadnehunk, the Allagash, the St. Lawrence, Gaspe, Natashquan). And always I wrote. When I turned thirty, I met the love of my life, married, committed myself to a serious job, and stopped writing. Well ... I stopped writing as a profession. Yet in a quiet moment, or while traveling and homesick for my wife, or camping in some far-out wilderness, I would fill the void by scribbling a poem or a short story on hotel notepaper or on a yellow legal pad. Upon retirement from my "serious" job, I learned it is possible to abandon a vocation but not possible to abandon an avocation. Last year it resulted in the publication of *We Escaped*, and now comes this selection from the poems I wrote over the years, some long ago, some recently. Surprisingly perhaps, those about death were mostly written when I was in my twenties, not now as I approach that finale. Two of the poems relate to a particular person and to a particular moment in time. "And Yet He Rots" was written a few hours after the assassination of President John F. Kennedy. "The Wakefield Bell" was written in the shadow of Virginia's Blue Ridge Mountains on the day of the inauguration of the bell now hanging in the Wakefield, New Hampshire, Congregational Church—a bell that was hung in memory of Joan Bozuwa, a remarkable young women who lived across the street from the church and who died while in her twenties, far too young, from (seemingly) a lightning strike of cancer.

When I was a freshman at college in New Hampshire, in 1956, my English literature professor invited Robert Frost to speak to our class. Frost at that time lived just across the New Hampshire state line in Vermont. (A few years later, Frost was appointed United States Poet Laureate by President John F. Kennedy.) Frost began his remarks to us by recounting that, many years before, he had been in the very same building we were sitting in at that moment. Like us, he was also a freshman, and he flunked his first courses, including English, during his first semester. He was separated from the college before Christmas of that freshman year and never returned to academia. He seemed amused, indeed proud of that accomplishment, tethered as it was to his illustrious career as a writer. Frost went on to say, "I have learned every poem has at least three meanings: the meaning of the author, that of the reader, and, in the instance of a class in literature"—he paused, shrugged, and smiled slyly in the direction of our professor—"the meaning of the professor." He winked and smiled again. "Whose meaning is of course paramount!"

Reading aloud has always been a pleasure for me. My children, my grandchildren, nursery schoolers, kindergarteners, and more recently fifth graders studying World War II who are amused by the sounds of the names of Dutch people, and of their towns and cities—reading to them is a joy. Cadence, volume, pitch, rhythm, tempo, what fun to toy with them! As when reading to those fifth graders a frightening paragraph about Dutch children, would-be escapees on skates nearing the Dutch/Belgian border, with everyone hanging on the whispered words—Would the children make their escape?—and suddenly bellowing *Halt!* in German so loudly, it can be heard at the other end of the school in the principal's office. Children starting from their seats with gasps of fright. And then astonishment, and then amusement. Such a yell! Out of place, simply not permitted in school. Yes, I enjoy reading aloud. And because I enjoy reading aloud, my poems are written not only for their meaning, but for their sound, their cadence, their movement. All my poems are meant to be read aloud.

Robert Frost was poking fun at our English professor when he assigned three meanings to every poem. He was not joking, however, about the underlying intent of his comments. Good poems inhere multiple levels of meaning. The more interpretations a poem suggests, the greater the joy in reading it. One can puzzle with the poem: sit in front of an open fire on a long winter night, sip a snifter of cognac, stare into the flames, and conjure up mysteries. Does the author really mean what he says? Or is he pulling my leg? Is death a finale, or a glorious beginning? A poem is good, in my view, when one wishes to read and reread it in order to better feel its rhythm, delight in its sound, and probe its meanings. And if it screams *Halt!* at some point, all the better.

As I write this foreword, death stalks one of the dearest friends of my family. It is painful to watch, excruciating to be helpless in the face of the inexorable march toward death. All one can do is love. This book is dedicated to her.

Alexander H. ter Weele
Caracole
May 2016

In Memory of

NANCY MERRITT

1948 – 2016

# TABLE OF CONTENTS

The Old Grist Mill 1

Ode 3

Take a Bow, Wear a Bow 5

Loneliness 7

Nowhere to Go 9

Let's 11

Birth 13

Little Squam 15

Dee diddle death 17

Touching, Feeling, Singing, Flying 19

A Stingy Beast Thou Art 21

Social Mores 23

Heavy Book, Heavy Read 25

What Time Is it? 27

Ringlets of the One I Love 29

And Yet He Rots 31

Dawn 33

ME and you 35

The Passion's Mine 37

Departure 39

Waves 41

Without Thee 43

Dreams Cannot the Living Touch 45

Death by Fire 47

On Loving and Parting 49

From the Void 51

Maples Turned to Fire 53

Life in the Forest 55

Heavenward 57

Tapestries of Silk 59

Good-bye 61

a cabin in winter 63

Happiness 65

Vox Clamantis 66

One Path through Time 68

Infinity 71

Essence 73

The Wakefield Bell 75

With the Wind at Your Back 77

## THE OLD GRIST MILL

Ah, Grist Mill! How I miss thee!
How I miss your spoons and cups,
How I pine to pass around the beers
And leer as customers smile "Cheers"
How I miss the chance to eye my dears ...
They're dears, those waitresses.

Ah, Grist Mill! How I miss thee!
How I miss your knives and forks,
How I pine to serve those dames in pearls
(Accompanied, alas, by churls).
How I miss the chance to eye the girls ...
Good girls, those waitresses.

Ah, Grist Mill! How I miss thee!
How I miss your food and plates,
How I pine to sweat within thy walls,
To tramp the length of your long halls,
Wear out my shoes and eye the dolls ...
They're dolls, those waitresses.

ODE

Wiser than the sphinx is she
With wisdom of eternity.
Is it thought? Or intuition?
Always right, her premonitions
About life.

Melancholy she can be
Or gayer than the chickadee.
Sometimes somber, perhaps sad
But mostly joyful and quite glad
With life.

Beauty's marked her, you can see;
She bears the signs of royalty.
Pharaoh's daughter? Egypt's queen?
The charms she has one had to preen
From life.

Love, I love to sing of thee
For thou art everything to me.
Wisdom, sadness, beauty, love,
Thou art the very essence of
My life.

### TAKE A BOW, WEAR A BOW

Three ducks in a boat, three ducks in a row;
Two ducks with paddles, one with a bow;
The first shot an arrow, two started to row.

The one with the arrow sat alone in the bow.
He chastised the others, he started a row.
Then, to soothe his companions he stood, took a bow.

Is it better to
row or stir up a row?
To shoot a bow or take a bow?
Better to row, or paddle and row?
Sit in the bow or wear a blue bow?

It's better by far
To wear a blue bow, to curtsy or bow,
Sit two in a row plus one in the bow,
Or paddle or row than to stir up a row.

LONELINESS

Music ripples, thoughts of you,
Lights soft, voices low.
Strangers murmur,
Reflections gleam,
Surroundings swell.
Nothing.

Carpets soft, sounds hushed,
Dark tones glimmer.
Polished wood, drapes surround.
Warmth, stillness.
Gentle breeding and contentment here.
Loneliness.

## NOWHERE TO GO

The way is weary, the road is hot and dry.
At times you travel on in solitude. Alone.
And then for days or even years the road is crammed
With carts and jostling crowds.
Sometimes you press on in haste,
Sometimes you lag and feel your load.
Stopping is forbidden,
The hordes scream "On! Move on!"
Go on.
Move on.
There is nowhere to go.

LET'S

Scratch a riddle huge or wee.
Shall we fiddle, you and me?
Why not ramble, scratch, and scramble?
Let us gambol, you and me.

Sing a jingle red or blue.
Shall we mingle me in you?
Why not jumble, fight, and fumble?
Let us tumble, me in you.

BIRTH

On a winter branch
A chickadee lilts its song
As spring approaches

LITTLE SQUAM

Warm sun. Wavelets lap the spiles of a wooden pier.
Sleeping in summer silence, Little Squam, virgin, untouched.
Dark hemlocks crowd the shore mixed with sugar maples, red oak, stands of white pine.
The aroma of wild woods, of serenity, of twinkling stars,
An aroma associated with New Hampshire, with silence,
With crystal-clear starry nights, with campfire smoke, with solitude.
An aroma that leads to dreams of peace, of quiet, of New Hampshire's forests.

Little Squam enraptures, a world away from the world.
A world made for the deer, the moose, the woodpeckers,
Woodpeckers that waken the woodlands each morning with their staccato thrumming.
A world made for the eerie night-wailing of loons, the disembodied cry of wilderness
That stirs the hair on the nape of one's neck, chills one to the tips of the toes.
A world wherein beauty caresses, a world we can love,
A world that slips away as summer dies, as our autumn nights lengthen.
A world we cannot own, a world that owns us,
A world we visit only briefly before we depart.

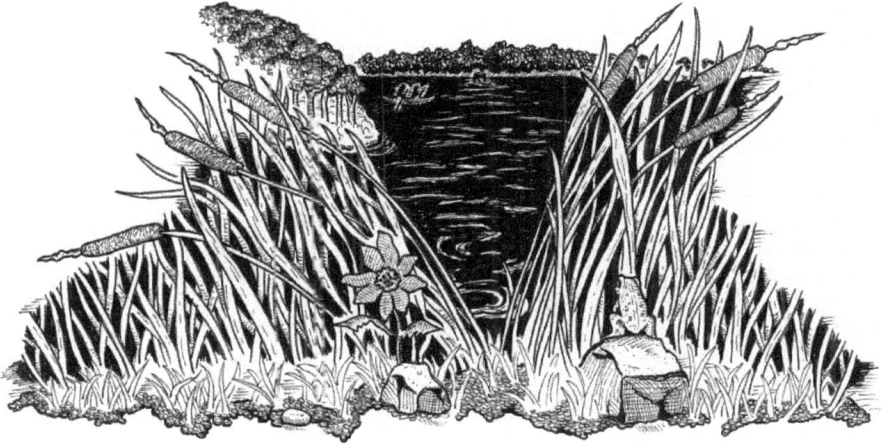

## DEE DIDDLE DEATH

Dee diddle diddle, cats cry and fiddle,
"The world is round and life a riddle."
Fly up, crawl down, laugh or frown, dress
                 in rags or wear a crown;
Yell or stammer, love or damn her, play exec or
                 pound a hammer.
Jump around, rest homebound; scream and kick or
                 make no sound.


EITHER        Think not at all and have a ball, break the law
                   and steal it all.
OR               Philosophize and eye your plight, keep the code,
                   do what's right.


          IT      MATTERS     NOT

You can't escape (there's no use crying)
Since you've been born, you,

           you've

                been

                     dying.

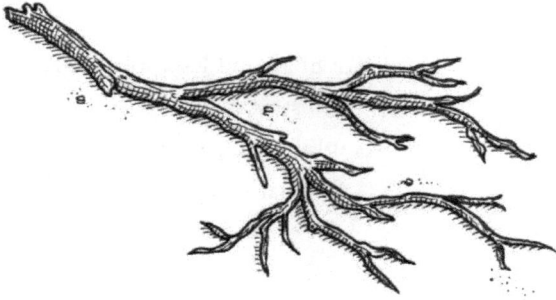

## TOUCHING, FEELING, SINGING, FLYING

The spring in bloom is what you are
The rising sun, a falling star
The warmth of seas in still lagoons
The piteous cry of long-lost loons.

When first we met, I sensed inside
A newfound warmth swell like a tide
Then recede, as do the seas,
To leave me bleak as leafless trees.

For you, I felt, were warm and near
You gave me love, dispelled my fear
Filled me with hope that humankind's
Replete with love in soul and mind.

That was the warmth, but then the chill
For what we had, now gone, is nil
The love and warmth and friendliness
Is past, has died: now loneliness.

Having met – and loved? – and then perceiving
Love has died begins the grieving
For touching, feeling, singing, flying
Then to lose it all – that's dying.

## A STINGY BEAST THOU ART

A stingy beast thou art, to give us life
While brandishing the knife to end it all.
We're given birth, then as we struggle on
You roll in mirth as our days die.
We feel your strength, a roasting fire.
We fight for length, those few days more
But all in vain. The heat we feel
Is just the flame: hot coals are yet to come.
You turn the spit. It would not do—
Would please no whit—should death be quick.
Thus life drags on, you in hysterics
While looking on our certain end.
The heat's turned high, your patience ends.
Escape? Why try? Your pleasure's o'er.

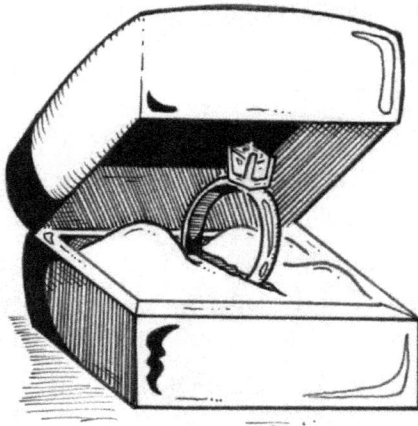

### SOCIAL MORES

What reason then? Why curb the yen
　Of single girls, unmarried men?
　　Are we afraid that man and maid
Will harm themselves in having strayed?

　Or do we fear that in a year
　Our social structure they will queer?
　　Do we foresee that he and she
　Will never wed if love's so free?

To me it's clear the day's not near
When marriage, poof!, will disappear.
　It's here today, it's here to stay
　Our social order's built that way.

So two in bed before they're wed
Won't strike our social structure dead.
　Our only fear, it thus is clear
Is that the man will harm his dear.

Or that the two someday will rue
The fun they had 'fore love was true.
　That fear I doubt; most people pout
They'd like more sex – but now they're stout!

　And others say, to be okay,
The marriage should have had foreplay.
　They seem to think, and write in ink,
　That virgin wedlocks simply stink.

So once again, why curb the yen
　Of single girls, unmarried men?

23

## HEAVY BOOK, HEAVY READ

This book, heavy as lead,
The one I love and now have read
Is not the one that teaches to lead
The one that I have yet to read.

And later, when I read
The one that teaches how to lead
I note it too is heavy as lead
Just like the one I already had read.

## WHAT TIME IS IT?

When green and orange turn to gray
    And fairy castles fade away
When neighbors' cats no longer roar
    And dreams of soldiers lead to war
When monstrous fish shrink in the pan
    And father's just another man

It's time to cry.


When love affairs are all alike
    When every walk becomes a hike
When work is done for Friday's pay
    And golden fields are seen as hay
When sleep is bought with bottled pills
    And dawn's first light torments the hills

It's time to die.

RINGLETS OF THE ONE I LOVE

Spring buds burst in wild array
As dawn exploding into day
With colors splashed across the sky
But summer heat soon sears the flowers
Just as the daylight overpowers
The dawn whose colors fade to naught.

Evening rays mass gold above
As ringlets of the one I love
Spread on a pillow, loose and gay....
But look away and gone the rays
The colors past as are the days
Spent idly with the one I loved.

### AND YET HE ROTS

Man snarls and snaps, jowls slaver
As he claws through putrid piles
Of fetid human flesh.
He rips and tears at those around,
Slashes at their throats with stinking fangs
Wrenches gonads from between wasted thighs.
He slobbers o'er the pus and maggots,
Gorges till his belly's bloated.
He pukes the human filth
Floods his lair with slime,
Gasps and gags in snot and emesis,
The soured mess sears his lungs.
He drowns in it; fangs rip at face and throat,
Blood bubbles down his front to where
Claws rip at balls and belly. He's dead, and
Yet he rots.

DAWN

Rising in glory
The sun descends in the west
Night dawns bright blackness

ME AND YOU

Humble grumble bumble bee; higgledy wiggledy look and see.
Crawl or fall, call a ball, you are short and me, I'm tall.
Brag of hag, nag a fag, chew the rag, or wave a flag,
**ME** I'm **BIG**

        (and
              you
                    you're
                          small).

**ME** a grumble, bumble crumble
You a wiggledy, tiggledy dee.
You look at you, I'll look at **ME**
For I am **HUGE**

        (and
              you
                   are
                       wee)

And all I see is me, Me, **ME!**

        Won t you look at me?

THE PASSION'S MINE

Her hair is black as ravens' wings
Her voice lilts soft as tinkling rings
Her cheek like down on bobwhite's breast
Her lips are blood-red rubies wrest
From passion's mine.

Her breasts are scented hyacinths
Her belly's creamy tinted chintz
Her thighs sleek panthers side by side
Her eyes like burning sapphires pried
From passion's mine.

DEPARTURE

Gone.

Gone the days of hunting together, and fishing,
Though hunting moved us both the most.
Gone the togetherness,
Although my solitary stalking draws me nearer to you.
Gone the sun on golden fields in autumn,
Gone the burst of wings, the rush of blood.
Perhaps it is the cold of winter fog which grips me
As I wait for dawn to break and stars to fade.
That call? A black lost on the lake?
Gone. Or do I feel a warmth in the rising of the sun?
I search the sky. No whisper of wings.

Silence.

Your call is clear. I hunt on, hoping that when I join you
Another will be left to hunt, to follow in our steps.
Will he hear the rush of wings as blacks descend in

Darkness?

WAVES

Swirling sloshing frothing playing
Whirling nipping foaming spraying
Whipping rearing flashing hurling
Banging crashing breaking bashing
Gripping slipping slurping sipping
Singing seething soothing seas.

## WITHOUT THEE

A speck of dust lies lonely in an empty field
A birch cracks cold in vast north woods.
A sun drifts ever through a boundless void
A straw bobs slowly on a swelling sea.
Thus, empty and forlorn, am I without thee.

## DREAMS CANNOT THE LIVING TOUCH

Myths,
Essence,
Incandescence
Snowflakes, netherness, and smoke
Shadows, lace, the white of Asian art
Mist and distant spires ...
Untouched, unreal, irrelevant.
Imagination cannot savor nectar's sweetness.
Unrequited, love is not;
Nor can dreams the living touch.

DEATH BY FIRE

On a winter branch
An icicle is hanging
It dies in the sun

ON LOVING AND PARTING

My chest's a cave of grief, love,
A cavern damp and dank;
My dreams would fill a sheaf, love,
My eyes see but a blank.

How hard it was to part, dear,
For love we had long shared;
You'd worked into my heart, dear,
My soul to you lay bared.

For months you were my life, love,
And all our ways were one.
You were to me my wife, love,
My moon, my stars, my sun.

And though our ways did part, dear,
And though our lives seem new,
You've shaped my mind and heart, dear,
Much, much of me is you.

To love and bid adieu, love,
To leave one's love behind
May seem much worse to you, love,
Than if love ne'er had shined.

But time will show, I own, dear,
That loving one another
Will blend in life a tone, dear,
We'd not trade for any other.

What we had and shared, love,
What we gave and got,
That which in us has flared, love,
Will rest fore'er ... our Camelot.

FROM THE VOID

Emptiness, solitude and void:
Whirling sun, long dead star, cold asteroid.
Nothingness, magnetic fields, an endless race.
Just space in me and me in space.
No thoughts, no aim, not even pain;
An ache within, no soul to stain.
Is it hurt? or lack of air?
Am I me or am I not?
Do I live? Can I be shot?
Can I be touched and can I touch?
Is life alone a life of much?
Or is it emptiness, and solitude, and void:
A whirling sun, a long dead star, an asteroid?
No! Life there is, alone or not,
To be conceived, pursued, and caught.
But from within this life is sprung
It isn't found but must be sung.
It must be welded, warmed, and forged
Created by us: then by us gorged.

MAPLES TURNED TO FIRE

The sky swings high above the trees,
Above the oaks and maples turned to fire.
The field grass dry and yellow,
Fringed by sumac berries tinged a
Darker crimson than the flaming woods.
A woodchuck squats fat on his burrow.
Slipping 'round on rising thermals the
Hawk cools while he watches.

life

i

nth

e

fores

t

is a

ing

ap      de

le           er

fleeing!

the
twangofthehunter's
bow

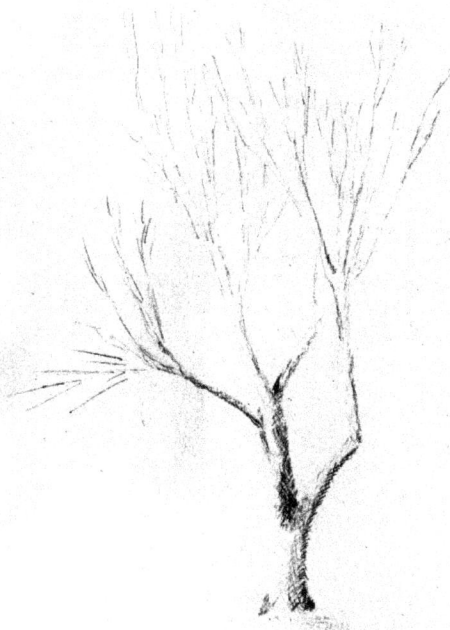

HEAVENWARD

Fluttering in wind
Crimson leaves tracing to earth
Heavenward spirals

## TAPESTRIES OF SILK

At times Life treats us royally.
She feeds us lotus leaves and honey,
Decks our beds in tapestries of silk;
Decorates our halls with gold and crystal chandeliers,
Tends our gardens filled with scents of myriad blossoms.

But then she, fickle as the early spring, takes revenge.
Gardens turn to sand and rock.
Great halls are charred and fall to enemy attack.
We are homeless; at night we toss on mats of thorns and nettles.
Parched throats are scratched by crusty bread.

She goads us now, cracks the whip as under
Searing sun our blistered feet ooze pus and blood.
We stumble in a quarry. Stumble and fall. Down.
The sun, a load of granite hard on our backs.
Dust in our throats, a swollen tongue …
She cracks the whip again.
We cannot rise.
She cackles.

GOOD-BYE

Hard it is to say good-bye
Hard to slip away, to die
Hard when birds sing, soar and fly
With sun and clouds bright in the sky.

Hard my wife to say good-bye
To never more beside you lie
Or dance and sing and with you fly
Hard to leave and not to cry.

Hard my sons to go, to die
When trout are rising to the fly
When grouse crouch tight about to fly
When campfire smoke wafts towards the sky.

Hard my daughter, hard to die
When children gathered 'round you try
To catch a frog or dragonfly.
When love for them lights in your eye.

Hard my family, hard to die
When birds sing, soar and fly
With sun and clouds bright in the sky
Hard to leave you all.
Hard not to cry.

a cabin in winter

winter woodland still and quiet
cabin lonely without sun
heavens gray enfold a promise
snow has fallen, snow to come

curling smoke wafts from the chimney
icicles in tempo drip
chickadees light on the feeder
suet fast and firmly grip

snowshoe tracks from woods to doorstep
mar the smoothness of the drifts
calling jay pretending anger
purposely the silence rifts

bite of axe resounding crisply
woodchips strewn about the snow
chipmunk twitching as he watches
perched nearby in some hedgerow

shadows lengthen in the gloaming
daylight dies a mournful death
owl hoots out across the woodland
anguished, sombrous, pensive breath

fire warm inside the cabin
shadows flicker on the wall
cricket creaking 'neath the wood box
thickening the hush o'er all

*HAPPINESS*

—ismuchtomanybuttomeis—

*LOVING YOU*

## Vox Clamantis

Come and bide by my grave in the gloaming
Hear my voice in the coming of dawn
As it whispers sweet words of endearment
Do not cry 'cause from here I am gone.

Won't you call out my name though I've left here
Do not weep though I've bid you good-bye
But remember my smile as I kissed you
And our love o'er the years now gone by.

Come and bide by my grave in the gloaming
Hear my voice in the coming of dawn
As it whispers sweet words of endearment
Do not cry 'cause from here I am gone.

As you sit here look out 'cross the valley
See the mountains rise blue to the sky
And think back to the time when we first met
And the years full of joy now gone by.

Come and bide by my grave in the gloaming
Hear my voice in the coming of dawn
As it whispers sweet words of endearment
Do not cry 'cause from here I am gone.

Can you hear Mistress Spring as she nears us
Does she warm the rich soil where I lie?
Are the woods full of flowers you planted
Do their blooms bring a tear to your eye?

Come and bide by my grave in the gloaming
Hear my voice in the coming of dawn
As it whispers sweet words of endearment
Do not cry 'cause from here I am gone.

Hear the birds in the trees as you doze here
While you dream of the life that we shared
Joie de vivre, exultation and laughter
From the children for whom we both cared.

Come and bide by my grave in the gloaming
Hear my voice in the coming of dawn
As it whispers sweet words of endearment
Do not cry 'cause from here I am gone.

## ONE PATH THROUGH TIME

One path through time from birth to death …
Regrets, regrets.

Narrow the path through time. Beautiful the forest it traverses.
So much to see, so many smells.
I woke today with deep regret at paths I had not traveled.
Most days the awe of my surroundings, the joy of stepping at a lively pace,
The companionship of those I meet along the way
Satiate my senses and bring great joy
And yet today …
Regrets.

So little time before I reach the summit, so many paths I might have taken
Sights I might have seen, loves I might have loved.
So little time.
So narrow a path.
So many other paths …
So many other paths …
Untraversed.

I am thirsty today while so many other days I have drunk deep
And stepped along the path giddy in the aftermath of wine.
Today my throat is parched. Regret.
Regrets for all the wine I might have drunk
Sadness at the wine we might have shared.
So little time before I reach the summit,
So many paths I might have taken, wines I might have tasted
Loves I might have loved.
So little time.
So many other wines we might have shared,
So many other wines ...
Untasted.


One path through time from birth to death.
One path, no more.


Regrets, regrets.

69

INFINITY

Ever rolling seas
Break upon the sands of time
Eternal thunder

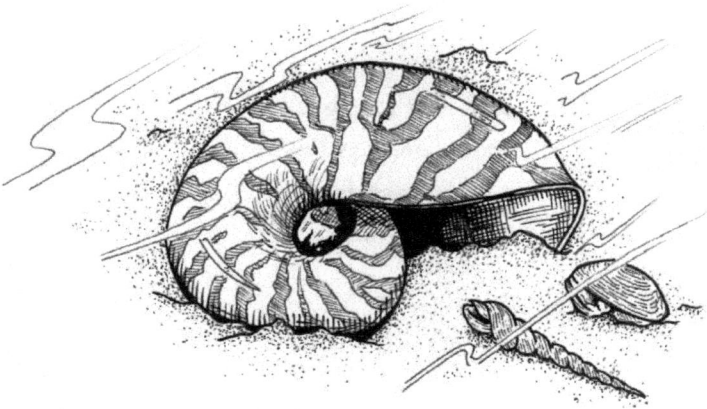

ESSENCE

You are the sun in me and more…
The dunes, the tides, the sea and shore
The mew of gulls, their lofty soar
The shells upon the ocean floor
The swell of waves, the breaker's roar…
The essence of the evermore
Are you.

## THE WAKEFIELD BELL

We woke this morning in Virginia to the peal of a bell which we had never heard before. Like a sea buoy tolling in a high wind or in a storm, the sound was sometimes faint, sometimes clear, sometimes caught away by the wind—difficult to say which tolls one heard and which one imagined, and difficult to say whether the sound came from a material bell or from one fashioned of more spiritual stuff.

The high notes of the bell echoed the laughter of a young girl playing with her brother, spoke of sunshine on her blond hair, of a kiss at bedtime for her mother, and of her smile as she sat on her father's knee. Happiness, amusement, beauty, curiosity, enthusiasm, love of life—the high notes of the bell spoke of these.

The carrying voice of the bell spoke of day-to-day love for family and friends—setting the breakfast table while half asleep to help mother, remembering to telephone father on his birthday, lending brother a hand with his homework, running an errand for a friend. Day-to-day love, thoughtfulness, kindness—the tolling of the bell spoke of these in certain, measured cadence. The certainty, the sureness, the regularity, the serenity of the love of which the bell tolled is the fabric Joan used to give life its meaning, hour by hour, day by day, and year by year.

The low tones of the bell which we heard spoke of tragedy, of sorrow, of loss. Yes, of tragedy and sorrow and loss, but not of bitterness. The low tones spoke also of acceptance and of giving; acceptance of death, made possible by the tenderness, support and love provided by father, mother, brother and friends; and giving, giving memories, insight, understanding, and, most importantly, giving a love which transcends death and of which the bell we hear will speak throughout the years across Wakefield, across the waters of Lake Wentworth and Winnipesaukee, through the passes and on the peaks of the White Mountains, along the Appalachias to Virginia, across the ocean to Holland, everywhere Joan has been and where her friends are.

The bell speaks to us of youth and of mirth, of tragedy and of death. But mostly it speaks to us of life, of love, and of Joan.

## WITH THE WIND AT YOUR BACK

May you always run, my son, with the wind
       at your back.
May your heart beat strong, fresh air fill your
         lungs, your stride be long and effortless.
May you run swiftly and far.
May you run with confidence and strength.
May luck run close by your side.

May you win many races, my son, and more:
May you run with determination those races
       which are unwinnable.
May you find the strength of leg to reach
       many finish lines,
And may you have the courage and will
        to run when you know that the
        finish line is beyond your reach.
May you always aspire to run, my son,
        to a further line, a line beyond
        the next turn, a line over the
        next hill, a line beyond the vision
        of the other runners in the race.

And in the greatest race of all, my son,
May you run with intelligence and grace,
       through pleasure and through pain.
May you have the courage to continue your run
        when others have abandoned the race
        and after your strength has failed you.

And at the end
May you have the fortune, my son, to die
       as I would die, running with
       concentration, your head high, your
       movements fluid, the next marker
       clearly in mind, and in full stride.

*Finis*